SPORTS STARS

STARS OF HOCKEY

by Matt Doeden

Consulting Editor: Gail Saunders-Smith, PhD

CAPSTONE PRESS
a capstone imprint

Pebble Plus is published by Capstone Press,
1710 Roe Crest Drive, North Mankato, Minnesota 56003
www.capstonepub.com

Library of Congress Cataloging-in-Publication Data
Doeden, Matt.
  Stars of hockey / by Matt Doeden.
     pages cm.—(Pebble plus. sports stars)
  Includes bibliographical references and index.
  Summary: "Simple text and full-color photographs feature eight current outstanding professional hockey players"—Provided by publisher.
  ISBN 978-1-4765-3960-7 (library binding)
  ISBN 978-1-4765-6025-0 (ebook PDF)
1. Hockey players—Biography—Juvenile literature. I. Title.
  GV848.5.A1D64 2014
  796.962092'2—dc23 [B]   2013030135

Editorial Credits
Erika L. Shores, editor; Sarah Bennett, designer; Eric Gohl, media researcher; Eric Manske, production specialist

Photo Credits
AP Photo: Gene J. Puskar, cover; Dreamstime: Leszek Wrona, 5, Rob Corbett, 21; Newscom: Icon SMI/Jeanine Leech, 7, 19, Icon SMI/Mark Goldman, 13, Icon SMI/Michael Tureski, 11, Icon SMI/Ric Tapia, 17, Icon SMI/YCJ/Andy Mead, 9, Reuters/Mike Blake, 15; Shutterstock: Lorraine Swanson, 1

Note to Parents and Teachers

The Sports Stars set supports national social studies standards related to people, places, and culture. This book describes and illustrates stars of professional hockey. The images support early readers in understanding the text. The repetition of words and phrases helps early readers learn new words. This book also introduces early readers to subject-specific vocabulary words, which are defined in the Glossary section. Early readers may need assistance to read some words and to use the Table of Contents, Glossary, Read More, Internet Sites, and Index sections of the book.

Printed in China by Nordica.
1013/CA21301922
092013   007747NORDS14

Table of Contents

Stars on Ice

He shoots. He scores!

Hockey fans cheer. They love

watching their favorite

NHL stars speed across the ice.

*NHL stands for
National Hockey League.*

Centers

Most hockey fans think center Sidney Crosby is the NHL's best player. Crosby can skate, pass, and score. He has more than 230 goals in the NHL.

Steven Stamkos is a rising star.

He scored 51 goals in

his second NHL season.

Two seasons later he topped

the NHL again with 60 goals.

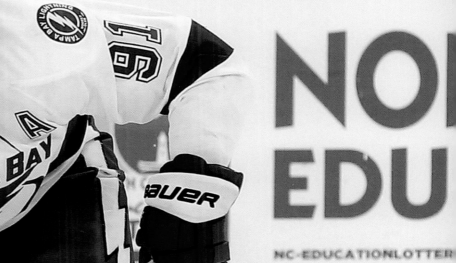

Evgeni Malkin is a star player.

He's scored more than 30 goals

in a season four times. He's

also won the Hart Memorial

Trophy as the NHL's top player.

11

Wings

Alex Ovechkin is a shooting machine. He had the most shots in the NHL in each of his first six seasons.

Corey Perry is an all-around
player. His 50 goals were
the most in the NHL one season.
He also has won a Hart
Memorial Trophy.

Twins Daniel and Henrik Sedin led the Vancouver Canucks to five straight division titles. Daniel is a wing. Henrick is a center.

Defensemen

Erik Karlsson is one of the NHL's best defensemen. He is a skilled passer. His 59 assists topped the NHL one season.

Fans call goaltender Henrik Lundqvist "King Henrik." He has led the NHL in shutouts twice. He holds a Vezina Trophy for being a top NHL goalie.

Glossary

assist—a pass that leads to a goal by a teammate

center—a player whose position is in the middle of the hockey rink

defenseman—a player whose main job is defense

division—a group of teams in the NHL; the NHL had six divisions in 2013

Hart Memorial Trophy—the award given to the NHL's most valuable player each season

shutout—a game in which a goaltender allows no goals

Vezina Trophy—the award given to the NHL's top goaltender each season

wing—a player whose position is on either the right or the left side of the hockey rink

Read More

Clay, Kathryn. *Cool Hockey Facts*. Cool Sports Facts. Mankato, Minn.: Capstone Press, 2011.

Greve, Tom. *Hockey Goalies*. Playmakers. Vero Beach, Fla.: Rourke Pub., 2010.

McClellan, Ray. *Hockey*. My First Sports. Minneapolis: Bellwether Media, 2010.

Internet Sites

FactHound offers a safe, fun way to find Internet sites related to this book. All of the sites on FactHound have been researched by our staff.

Here's all you do:

Visit *www.facthound.com*

Type in this code: 9781476539607

Index

Word Count: 216
Grade: 1
Early-Intervention Level: 18